BLOOMSBURY
REFLECTIONS

[signature] '97

BLOOMSBURY REFLECTIONS

ALEN MACWEENEY

SUE ALLISON

with a foreword by
FRANCES SPALDING

W·W·NORTON & COMPANY
NEW YORK · LONDON

ISBN 0-393-02906-9

W. W. Norton & Company, Inc
500 Fifth Avenue, New York, N.Y. 10110
W.W. Norton & Company, Ltd
10 Coptic Street, London WC1A 1PU

Printed in Great Britain

1 2 3 4 5 6 7 8 9 0

First published in Great Britain 1990 by
Ryan Publishing Co Ltd
London

Frontispiece
VIRGINIA BELL
*with a bust of her great-aunt Virginia Woolf by Stephen
Tomlin and a painting of Adrian Stephen
by Duncan Grant, Charleston.*

ACKNOWLEDGMENTS

The authors wish to thank the people in this book for their generosity in allowing us to photograph and interview them, often at some length.

To Christopher Naylor and the staff of the Charleston Trust, Reverend Vicary House of Berwick Church and Peter Mile of the National Trust who all extended themselves and facilitated our endeavours to complete this book.

The photographer is indebted; to Life; to Carol Fondé whose sensitive eye and determination brought an enviable refinement to the colour printing of the photographs; to Baldev Duggal and Sethu Raja of Duggal Color Projects for their generous contributions and; to the unseen assistance of Brian Coats and Robert Feldman.

LIST OF PLATES

FOREWORD

One of the themes in Virginia Woolf's To the
Lighthouse *is the transformation of chaos into shape, the
momentary into the permanent. The celebrated dinner
party given by Mrs Ramsay begins with disparate
individuals making polite conversation over a bedrock of
disorder and internal strife. 'Life, which shot down even
then from this dining-room table in cascades,' Mrs Ramsay
observes, amid distracting thoughts about people she has
known in the past, the present behaviour of her children
and her husband's anger at the request of one guest for
more soup, does not at that moment bend to her desire.
Then the candles are lit, the boeuf en daube is served, the
conversation runs in fresh channels and the guests begin to
coalesce. Suddenly Mrs Ramsay, searching in the pot for
an especially tender piece of meat for the elderly Mr Bankes,*

senses 'a coherence in things, a stability; something, she meant, is immune from change .... Of such moments, she thought, the thing is made that remains ever after. This would remain'.

When we pick up a camera, to record a place, event, a moment within family life or the meeting of friends, we are, in effect, trying like Mrs Ramsay to say, 'Life stand still here'. The results may be disappointingly inadequate, and too fragmentary for us to share with Lily Briscoe, the painter who towards the end of To the Lighthouse is inspired by her memory of Mrs Ramsay to complete a picture, the realisation that the moment has been 'struck into stability'. Even so, snapshots housed in a photograph album and rediscovered years later have an extraordinary charge, in part because as time passes they accrue more layers of memory and sentiment. The single, mechanical eye of the camera, precisely because it is so tied to the here and now, serves the future with its powerful ability to bring us close to the past.

In the case of Alen MacWeeney's photographs we are presented with images that bear comparison with the photo-portraits of Bill Brandt, Felix H. Man and Jane Bown in their ability to distil the quintessence of a sitter's character or mode of life. It is not only his sensitivity to pose, light and composition that gives these photographs such holding power, but also the way that colour, which can be disruptive in its easy seductiveness, is harnessed to his purpose with eloquence and restraint. But these photographs are not merely the product of great technical and formal skill. They also bring into operation correspondences and allusions that echo backwards in time. For those familiar with the history of Bloomsbury they will create a confluence of sensations, as our response to the immediacy of the sitter's presence combines with awareness of things more remote.

There is, for instance, an intriguing play upon hereditary relationships in one photograph taken in the studio at Charleston. Hovering within the silvery surface of an old mirror is the sharply lit reflection of Virginia Bell, which presses forward behind the bust of her great-aunt Virginia Woolf by Stephen Tomlin. To the left is Duncan Grant's portrait of Virginia Woolf's brother, Adrian Stephen, in whose face there is sufficient likeness to return us once again, with more questioning gaze, to Virginia Bell's reflection. The association of these three heads may serve as a reminder that all are descended from the Pattle sisters, famous for their beauty, and one of whom, Julia, became the second wife of Sir Leslie Stephen, great-grandfather of Virginia Bell.

A similar density of association can be found in the photograph of Frances Partridge. She is shown seated at her writing table in her Belgravia flat, beneath Duncan

Plate 2
DESMOND MacCARTHY'S GRANDCHILDREN
Jonathan Cecil, Desmond MacCarthy, his sister Mary Brettingham-Smith, and Hugh Cecil.

Grant's The Jugglers, a painting that formerly hung at Ham Spray, the house where Ralph and Frances Partridge lived after the deaths of Lytton Strachey and Carrington. On the right is a small sketch by Vanessa Bell of a baby's head. The baby in question is Henrietta Garnett who was to marry Frances Partridge's son, Burgo. These and other items that surround her allude to her past life and present occupation as a writer and amateur musician. But it is the copy of her autobiography, Memories, on the left-hand side of the table that offers a clue to the whole, for, like other of her books, it upholds a fusion of intelligence with sensibility which this quietly dignified portrait so eloquently displays in the sitter's face.

The intimacy in these portraits is nicely guarded. We enter George Rylands' bedroom in his rooms at King's College, Cambridge, to find him waiting at the ready. Henrietta Garnett relaxes on the laundry box at Charleston with a feline composure. Nigel Nicolson turns towards us in his chair with interrogatory stare. For Mac-Weeney, it seems, is very alert to the irony inherent in photography's dependence on artifice for natural effects. Now and then his photographs show a sympathy with Vanessa Bell's belief, as reported by her son Quentin, that the subject matter of photography should be a little absurd. When making this remark she may have had in mind the photographs taken by her great-aunt, Julia Margaret

Cameron, who posed her sitters in a 'high-art' mode, and whose aim was not merely to 'take' photographs but to immortalize those dragooned into posing for her. Of the Pattle sisters, she was the least beautiful. 'A woman of noble plainness', the painter, G. F. Watts politely remarked, making no mention of the stink of chemicals that clung to her person.

When Vanessa Stephen moved with her sister and two brothers into 46 Gordon Square in 1904, she hung a row of Mrs Cameron's photographs of eminent Victorians down one side of the hall, opposite another row which were all of her mother. The Stephen sisters had themselves begun using a camera prior to this date, and it remained an important tool in their lives, documenting holidays in the country or by the sea, Bloomsbury antics and a host of visitors. Our knowledge of Bloomsbury's contribution to social history has been in no small measure enhanced by the two picture-books compiled from Vanessa Bell's and Lady Ottoline Morrell's photograph albums. Many others who visited Charleston, Monk's House, Ham Spray or other Bloomsbury haunts, brought cameras with them, not least Lettice Ramsay, a girlfriend of Julian Bell, who set up as a professional photographer in Cambridge and recorded likenesses of some of the most brilliant minds of this century.

Alen MacWeeney's images form an outstanding coda to

Plate 3
THE STUDIO, CHARLESTON
Fireplace by Duncan Grant, tiles by Vanessa Bell.

the photographic history of Bloomsbury. In their subtle manipulation of colour and light they seem to admit a debt to the painter's example and therefore seem especially sympathetic to the decorations at Charleston. They can also be seen to extend the dialogue between painting and photography which allowed Vanessa Bell and Duncan Grant, in their later years, to use photographs as source material for their art. As can be seen in the plate showing the Bell family at Charleston, photographs litter the mantle-piece and contribute to the creative clutter of the studio. All MacWeeney's photographs draw us in and invite lengthy attention. The people that appear in this book are all either friends of those who formed the original core of Bloomsbury, or their descendants. Some may nowadays claim very little affinity with the values and beliefs that Bloomsbury shared. But one cannot fail to notice an adamantine resoluteness in the faces that appear here, for all seem to have been touched, either by association or through descent, with an inheritance they cannot forget.

FRANCES SPALDING

BLOOMSBURY REFLECTIONS

FRANCES PARTRIDGE

Since her husband, Ralph, whom she called Rafe, died in 1960, Frances Partridge has made her home in a one-bedroom flat in London where, surrounded by paintings by Vanessa Bell and Duncan Grant, she has written two Bloomsbury memoirs, compiled two volumes of her diaries and continues to write the occasional book review.

They were definitely left wing. This is 'Old Bloomsbury' that I'm talking about. They were pacifists at the time of the First World War. There were several conscientious objectors among them – James Strachey and David Garnett and Duncan Grant and so on. But come the Second World War, they seemed to have altered. And Rafe was just the other way around. He went straight into the army. Indeed, he hardly knew the Bloomsburys until he came out. And he did frightfully well. But the war left him completely disillusioned. In the Second War, although he was too old to fight, he stood as a conscientious objector, and I think that was rather better than what the others did, really, because when they were too old to fight, they rather supported the idea of other young men going to the war.

Plate 4
FRANCES PARTRIDGE

They put relations before conventions. Marriage, divorce and all that parcel they thought they didn't need. They believed that the relations themselves were more important than the laws controlling them. As with other things, I don't think they did it very deliberately. Most of the oldest members of Bloomsbury, like Leonard, Desmond MacCarthy and Clive Bell, had been at Cambridge with G. E. Moore, so it had all been very much in the air there.

Lytton was the intellectual of the group. He was very, very influential at Cambridge, evidently. He was always ready to laugh, and the jokes weren't always the cleanest. There were lots of obscenities mixed in, and games. I think he rather liked to shock. He could be very kind, too.

We would have fascinating arguments and conversations. Bloomsbury liked arguing, and that's one thing I liked: discussion. They liked talking about abstract subjects and general ideas instead of just endless gossip. Virginia's conversation was amazing. She would be like a bonfire that suddenly catches light. She'd go up up in a great flight of words and fantasies sometimes, and fun. I think people think of Bloomsbury as more solemn than it was. There was a great deal of laughter and jokes. But certainly sometimes the arguments were quite heated. People now talk about the Bloomsbury Group, but they never would have then. They were just friends, and friends never agree on everything. But agreeing wasn't the point. They argued for the mere stimulation of it.

They stayed friends out of sheer affection. They did share this outlook, this general view that they were going their own way. They were awfully amused by each other. They made tremendous fun at each other sometimes. Roger Fry, for instance, was a delightful man, but he had his curious habits. He was a tremendous believer in quack medicines. I believe he was called 'Old Credulity' in the picture trade. But he was a brilliant critic, and it was marvellous to attend his lectures, and he was a very, very charming, kind man; very sympathetic. Duncan was incredibly charming. He didn't seem to have to try. Everybody loved him.

Virginia could be wonderfully kind and sensitive to people in trouble. She was very kind to me, for instance, after the deaths of Lytton and Carrington when Rafe was terribly upset. We had desperately tried to prevent Carrington from committing suicide after Lytton's death. We knew she meant to. I don't recommend that situation to anyone: that is anguish. And Rafe failed so he felt desperate. I remember going to Charleston from there and Virginia was suddenly so kind to me. When we were being driven back, she sat beside me in the car and she said all the nicest things she could – affectionate things. I think she meant them at the time. But she could hit people off with great malice and description. Many people were wounded by what she wrote in her diary, I think.

She was a hypersensitive person. Of course, her brilliance comes partly from that. The least thing would upset her. I think the people who think it odd that the Hogarth Press published Freud's works and yet that Virginia herself never underwent psychoanalysis forget how early her madness began. It was long before Freud became at all popular over here. They started to publish his works in 1922. I know because I did the index for the blooming thing. But the public interest in Freud may have begun in the 'twenties, and by then, Virginia had had almost all of her mad fits, because she had very long absolutely sane periods. But she went to the specialists in the mad. Leonard consulted all the best specialists. The practitioners here thought it was very dangerous to treat the mad, to psychoanalyze them, because you might stir them up and drive them into a madness. I think Leonard's total devotion to her and all the trouble he took with her must not be questioned. He did everything that was at that time do-able, and in a way as she grew older she steadied, and it was just these times when a book was published – she was full of terrible doubts and that I think gave her her bouts of madness after a book came out: the strain of finishing it and waiting to see what the critics would say – and the war. Every bout of her madness had a cause. The earliest ones were her mother's death and the death of her stepsister, and possibly marriage because she obviously couldn't face sex.

If anybody ever asked me who was the cleverest man I ever met I would say Maynard. He had these brilliant eyes. He wasn't a handsome man, but he was a man of enormous charm. His eyes shone with the brilliance of thought and you felt that anything he said was brilliant, though I never heard him talking about a serious thing. He was very interested in painting. He bought a lot of it. He encouraged the interest in the Impressionists. He had to go over to the peace conference in Paris at the time when nobody else had gone – just after the war – and had seen those paintings there. He also had a great taste for the ballet. That's how he met his wife. Writers say he was homosexual, but they'd better think again and say bi-sexual; he and Lydia Lopokova were most devoted.

Work was terribly important to the Bloomsburys. They worked for the love of work and the interest of it. The painters went on painting even when nobody wanted to buy their pictures. And they used to sit in the garden a lot. The flowers seemed to grow bigger in Charleston than any other garden. I went there quite often. Clive asked me down. I had happy times there. And other people would go there – Roger Fry, the MacCarthys. Desmond was a great social lion. He had enormous Irish charm and he was a wonderful talker: he would listen, and bring people out. Grand ladies liked to have him at their dinner tables. Molly was really very brilliant, and in a way wrote a better letter than Desmond, but she was very deaf and so didn't get asked out. But they would be by at Charleston. Clive liked having Desmond for dinner. Clive loved having talk around the dinner table.

I spent my life among these people. Every other member is dead, I think. I really do feel a bit of a dodo now. Well, Dadie Rylands is my generation, and Nigel Nicolson – his father was a great friend of Clive's, who was a great friend of mine. They were intimidating, but of course in a way it was so fascinating that one tended to forget one's foolishness. And they were very kind. I was young then, and they were very kind.

Plate 5
GEORGE RYLANDS
with photographs of himself as Lady Macbeth.

GEORGE 'DADIE' RYLANDS

In 1927, at the age of twenty-five, George Rylands began his sixty year career as a Cambridge University don, specializing in all aspects of the works of William Shakespeare. But before his eminent academic career began, he went to London, to work for Leonard and Virginia Woolf at the Hogarth Press.

The first Bloomsburys I met, properly, were Lytton Strachey and Carrington. Lytton was a very very great friend of my classical tutor, J. T. Shephard, who eventually became Provost here and who was a very great friend to me. He and Lytton had been undergraduates and Apostles together. I was an Apostle in those far-off days. Lytton and Shephard were very devoted friends, so when Lytton came to Cambridge, while I was an undergraduate, I was introduced to him, and then when I became an Apostle we became great friends. I started going to stay at Ham Spray quite soon after he and Carrington had moved from Tidmarsh. I would stay with them on weekends, see Lytton when he came here. Then he took me to Rome for ten days holiday. All of the Stracheys were very very peculiar and gifted and interesting and clever and wonderful and slightly off-centre. Lytton was more amusing than you could think possible. His physical health was generally not good, and he was very emotional, so his personal relations could make him melancholy, but he was an enjoyer. He loved music and friends and eating. His reading aloud was an absolute delight to listen to. And then I got to know Carrington. I became a devoted friend of beloved Carrington. Knowing her was very special. She has been much overlooked. She was a great painter, and a wonderful letter-writer. When I came to Cambridge, I said to her, 'I'm coming to these great bleak rooms and have no possessions and it's very very chilly and I have nothing but a bit of china so will you come and decorate it?' And she did, in 1928, or 1929.

Maynard Keynes was very important, and of course it was more fascinating

Plate 6
GEORGE RYLANDS
in his bedroom at King's College.

because he married a ballet dancer. He made King's College quite a rich college. When I came up as an undergraduate, we were a very poor college. When I came back as a fellow, owing to Maynard's manipulations of properties, as bursar, with a certain recklessness and brilliance, we were a fairly rich college.

He was slightly odd man out among the Bloomsburys, although he was a very close friend of them all. He was a man of the world, which they slightly mistrusted, with a hint of mockery. He was rich, thanks to his financial skill, which they were not, and he was a pre-eminent public servant, especially in World War II at the Treasury. He went with the head of the Treasury for one of the great loans after the war. He was already a very sick man and oughtn't to have gone and it was a terrific strain dealing with all the Treasury officials and what not in the great United States and when he came back, he expired. He had a heart attack and died. He wasn't very old. He hadn't reached seventy. But he had been overworked all through the war, and when he really had to struggle to try and save the failing finances of Great Britain, it did him in, really.

Apart from all his great economics work, for which his name is still internationally famous, he wrote several delightful studies, and he initiated what became the Arts Council of Great Britain. But he had a passion for the theatre. About 1934, he confided in me his desire to give Cambridge a theatre, and he asked me to cooperate. This gave him more pleasure than anything in the last ten years of his life. He was a very special friend and colleague. I knew him from my first term here, when he asked me to luncheon.

The most remarkable thing about them all was their wit – their wit and humour, and the fact as a group they were very special. Being individual within their group was one thing, but also as a group they were very special. Just as one could say, looking back at the Pre-Raphaelites – the whole group of eccentric people from Oxford in the 1850's; William Morris and all that – so Bloomsbury stood for something. And it was really a Cambridge affair. It was entirely a Cambridge affair.

They were very influenced by the fact that Cambridge is not fashionable like Oxford and is a good, Puritanical, intellectual, middle-class university, whereas at

Oxford the students all become prime ministers and ambassadors and they all have money. Cambridge is a very out-of-the-way, old-style, evangelical, serious world. And they were all Apostles, which is a tradition that still goes on and which carries on the kind of feeling that you can and should say anything you want to say. Freedom. Total freedom of speech and freedom of thought. Not being bound. Their intellectual training, that of the chief ones, came in Cambridge. With that intellectual foundation, they began to question everything and to revolt against the whole Victorian affair. And then they happened to have several very brilliant people, both in painting and writing, among them. They became great friends, several of them. Of course, they broke up for a time because Leonard went off to Ceylon as a civil servant, but then he married Virginia. They really were a group of friends. It was a very special friendship, but it was based, ultimately, on Cambridge and the Cambridge way of thought.

Whatever was written against them was written out of envy and hostility. If anything is a group, if anything is a success, then people think, 'Oh, they're so frightfully pleased with themselves.' And in a way they were. And why not? If you have something to be pleased about. The curious thing is that even clever Oxford people who admired Duncan and Roger very much were still hostile to Cambridge. If you mention any Bloomsbury affair to an Oxford man or woman, they would turn their noses up. I think we all admire Oxford because they're so frightfully successful and so smart and so good-looking and so rich, et cetera. So we all think Oxford is simply wonderful. And Oxford thinks the same! Of course, you may say that Cambridge thinks that they're clever and intellectual and they are, and they do!

JOHN LEHMANN

It wasn't until the young poet and Cambridge undergraduate John Lehmann came to work for them in 1931 that Leonard and Virginia finally had an apprentice they felt they could trust. He started in 1931 and when he left after eighteen months to start his own literary magazine, New Writing, he was not replaced and when he returned, in 1938, it was as a full partner. In 1946, Lehmann left again, to begin his own publishing company. He died in 1987.

We had conflicts, Leonard and I, but I was always very fond of him. There was something sympathetic about him. Even so, I could never forget that he was a brilliant intellectual and in the fore of supporting such writers as T. S. Eliot.

The centre of his life was Virginia. He would get into the most fearful stew if Virginia took a walk in London without telling him. He would become agitated, worried about her. I think it is possible to say that if he hadn't been so attached to Virginia he may have done a lot more writing. But maybe not. He had great socialist interests, political interests, and of course publishing interests. Besides the Hogarth Press, he was very much the chap behind the *Political Quarterly*, the Labour Party magazine.

They were both very important to me, but Virginia was particularly so. I admired her and worshipped her. Artistically and spiritually her novels and writing meant more to me than did the work of anyone else in that generation. She was enormously curious and inquisitive. She liked one to talk about one's friends. She liked one to be indiscreet, mostly. She loved gossip. Of the two, I was closest to Virginia because she allowed me to be close. She would support me in my conflicts with Leonard, with whom I had a dual relationship in both senses of the word.

It was great fun helping people realize their writing. Writers need someone to help them. Not Virginia, though. Virginia was absolutely a phenomenon by herself.

Plate 7
JOHN LEHMANN

HENRIETTA GARNETT

The daughter of David and Angelica Garnett – and granddaughter of Duncan Grant and Vanessa Bell – Henrietta married her childhood idol, Burgo Partridge, the only son of Ralph and Frances Partridge, when she was just seventeen. Less than a year later, Burgo died suddenly of a heart attack, leaving Henrietta to raise their infant daughter, Sophie Vanessa. Now working on her second novel – her first, Skeletons in the Closet, *was published in 1986 – Henrietta lives in France. Sophie, who, like her mother, married at seventeen, lives on a sheep farm in Tuscany with her husband and their two little girls.*

I simply can't imagine not having known them, because I always knew them. It was utterly delightful. I wasn't at all conscious in my childhood that they were especially famous. When I was twelve one of my father's novels was published and it was a book we had to read for our school examinations and I got funny looks from the kids. But in the 1950s, Bloomsbury was not in fashion, and they weren't known. We were very poor.

We used to go to Charleston on our holidays. It was quite demanding. We had to work. We had to stand stock still after breakfast, posing for the painters. I was always happy there. They were happy because they had the luck to love working and they loved what they worked at: Vanessa and Duncan at painting and Clive at writing. I was always surrounded by beauty there, and by conversation of the highest calibre. I knew they were different, and I enjoyed them tremendously.

Plate 8
HENRIETTA GARNETT
on a linen chest decorated by Duncan Grant, Charleston.

We considered Charleston heaven, my sisters and I. It was a treat to go there, and a pity to leave. Nessa, Clive and Duncan were living there, and the cook and their son, and sometimes Quentin would be there. Vanessa had frugal habits. For lunch, we would have ham, boiled potatoes and a salad made by Duncan. We had dessert at lunch, but none at dinner. Clive always made you feel more intelligent than you really were. He taught me a great deal. How to shoot pheasant. Why he would hesitate to buy a Degas. He always treated us as if we were adults. He always wanted us to be intelligent, amusing.

Vanessa was an extremely distinguished woman of remarkable intelligence, and even though she was old, she was astonishingly beautiful. She had a lovely voice, and a loving expression. She twinkled when she smiled. But she could be severe if you didn't own up to having done something wrong. She would give you a dire look. I was sixteen when Vanessa died. I wasn't her favourite grandchild, but she had a curious affection for me. I looked like and had the same character as Duncan. I never knew he was my grandfather until I was seventeen. It was when I was engaged to Burgo that my father told me, and he said that I would not be lucky. But it came as no surprise. I think I always knew. It was always 'Nessa and Duncan', 'Nessa and Duncan'. It was never 'Nessa and Clive'. My reaction when I found out was delight and pride, and gratitude to Clive. He couldn't have been a nicer pretence grandfather.

I can't describe Duncan, but sometimes I feel like him. I once asked him if he believed in magic, meaning God, but not wanting to mention God. He said, 'Yes, but it's better not to talk about it'. When I was twelve, I decided to become a Buddhist and outraged everyone in my family, who were all atheists. Everyone except Duncan. He was very credulous. He was so innocent. He didn't know about sin.

Plate 9
QUENTIN BELL

Plate 10
CRESSIDA AND VIRGINIA BELL

Plate 11
JULIAN AND SOPHIE BELL

QUENTIN BELL

When Quentin Bell's biography of his aunt, Virginia Woolf, was published in 1972, it was an immediate bestseller. The only surviving son of Clive and Vanessa Bell (his older brother, Julian, was killed in the Spanish Civil War in 1937), Quentin became a potter, university teacher and writer. He lives in Sussex, not far from Charleston, with his wife, Olivier, editor of Virginia's famous diary.

Other people walk through the rooms of Charleston and imagine a Bloomsbury of their own, whereas I just knew people. They imagine it was full of characters who spent all their time in brilliant, high-powered discussion when they actually spent their time eating, working, smoking and sitting. It was not a brilliant society. There were one or two brilliant talkers. Maynard Keynes was dazzling. Desmond MacCarthy had a kind of warmth and wit which was wonderful. Some of them spent an awful lot of time being silent. Every now and then you would hear a groan, or an obscenity. Painting is a silent art. I'm not sentimental about Charleston. I just think of it as an interesting and fascinating place. It's a nice place to be. It's not a melancholy house. The main thing about the house is it has a lovely light, so it was a good house for painters.

I was very fond of both of my parents. They were very nice people. They were very different from each other. My mother used to run things. She ran the house because no one else wanted to. But she escaped. Critics dismiss my father with a sneer, but they are wrong. He had great social gifts. He was a good father. My brother didn't get on with him. Clive liked society, and was close to it. He did like duchesses, which Julian, who was a socialist, definitely didn't. Clive had some money. My mother was not interested in money. She was only interested in having enough to keep the children alive. They were not in the business for money. They wanted to be happy in life. They didn't want to be rich. My father didn't work very hard, but my mother and Duncan Grant were miserable if they couldn't paint from

Plate 12
THE BELL FAMILY

eight in the morning until eight in the evening. We didn't see her unless we posed for a painting. My children earned 6d for an hour.

The people who turned up at Charleston put up with us brats extraordinarily well. We would put bombs in the garden and never got a word of reproach. My first memory of Maynard Keynes was on a small boat trip across the river. He had a straw hat, which was called a boater. I was struck by the name of the hat and so I whizzed it across the water to see if it would float. It did. I thought it was a very satisfactory experiment. He never said anything about minding.

They were a very nice lot, these characters. Lytton spent a lot of time despairing. He enjoyed despairing so much. But in point of fact, he knew that you knew he was an old fraud. He was beaming with contentment most of the time. Bloomsbury were always regarded by the press as the most horrible people. The press said Virginia Woolf was an affected, snobbish, upper-class lady. In a sense, the press got it right about Bloomsbury. They realized fundamentally what Bloomsbury was about and they attacked them for their ideas, and they did assess some of the attitudes precisely. But there was great animosity and that was partly prejudice against them, which we still suffer. When I was born, there was an exhibition in London of paintings by Cézanne, Matisse and Picasso. The devil in this situation was Roger Fry, who was all the time plugging Cézanne, saying he was the greatest painter who ever lived. People hated Cézanne and all the Post-Impressionists but Bloomsbury were great supporters. That is the kind of thing that breeds ill-will.

CRESSIDA BELL

One of Quentin and Olivier Bell's three children, Cressida Bell is a textile designer in London.

From the time I was four we would spend our summer holiday in France and we would always go to Charleston for a week, either on the way to France or on the way back. We loved it there. The adults would talk about Bloomsbury, but just in the way that people talk about the old days. Someone might tell a story, or show a picture of Dadie Rylands and my parents would say, 'Oh, do you remember the time when Dadie...?' Or someone would say, 'Nessa would do that...' That's how it would happen. They wouldn't sit around reminiscing. It was just conversations like anyone would have talking about friends.

What I remember most is leaving the grown-ups after lunch and going on long walks in the downs. You could walk up and see it raining below you and we used to get stuck in the mud on a regular basis in the road that went past the farm. We would get absolutely stuck and we would stand there and yell. We didn't go to the studio much. One didn't want to disturb Duncan. He was always in the studio working or reading. That was his room.

Grace would make the lunch and the bell was rung and we would go into the dining room and sit down and it was all there. Grace's kitchen was one of the focal points for the children. We had the garden but if nothing was happening we'd go into the kitchen and talk to Grace: see if we could help her, lick out the cake bowl, or whatever. She was very central to Charleston. I can't remember what Clive was doing there then. I remember that he always used to come into lunch last. He had one of those collars around his neck. He was a pretty elderly gent. To me he was just sort of a slightly distant old man. Duncan was very sort of lively and jolly and when we moved to Sussex we saw a lot of Duncan. He came to dinner every Saturday. He came at Christmas.

My point of contact with Quentin through my teenage years was going to the pottery with him. I used to put on my wellies and go off to Charleston. Quentin would pot and Duncan would paint and Quentin would teach me how to throw pots. It was quite fun.

Plate 13
ANGELICA GARNETT'S LIVING ROOM

Plate 14
ANGELICA GARNETT

ANGELICA GARNETT

Angelica Garnett is the daughter of Vanessa Bell and Duncan Grant. She was married to the writer David Garnett – called Bunny – a man more than twenty years her senior for twenty-five years and had four children.

There is a recording of Virginia's voice and even to me, although I recognize it, it comes as a shock each time I hear it. It's very deep and you hear all her timidity, all her fear – she was obviously petrified in front of the microphone – and all her formality. You hear two things: one, that it is her voice and very characteristic, but you also hear a lot of overtones of nervousness which weren't there in normal conversation. She was actually somebody who found it quite easy to be intimate. She had immense funds of affection and love for people. This came out mostly in family relationships so that with me she was tremendously lively and affectionate and I never felt that she was 'The Famous Aunt', at all. Her fame wasn't a very important thing. In those days fame was so much smaller and her own fame was minuscule compared to what it is now. She couldn't have coped with all the people who would come to her now, wanting her to lecture or be photographed. In those days, although that happened a bit, it was something she could handle and something we didn't talk about a great deal and that she on principle thought that you shouldn't talk about too much, anyway. She thought it was a nuisance in many ways but she didn't let it get inside her in any way that it altered her writing. She had great strength of character and personality. Her actual moral strength was terrific, much more important than her madness.

Bunny was a very warm human being and he loved relationships with all kinds of people. He had a very wide spectrum of friends so it was very exciting meeting them all. But like Vanessa, he was also very possessive and he also had a very, very strong personality and a very strong willpower. Marrying him was like jumping out of the frying pan into the fire.

My husband told me about having been lovers with Duncan. But he made it sound very much more casual and less consenting on his part than I have now come to the conclusion that it was. I was frightfully innocent. I thought homosexuality was a physical thing, which I didn't care for the idea of at all. I didn't know about the implications: what it might mean for Duncan's daughter to marry his lover.

I eventually became very close with my father, especially after my mother died. But he never gave me a fatherly feeling. He was not a natural father but he was a gently warm person. He was an amazing man, absolutely extraordinary. He never interfered in other people's existences. He always let them do exactly what they wanted. Everybody loved Duncan. People felt safe with him. They knew he wouldn't do anything to hurt them. He loved people. He was very affectionate but he was not passionate. He never went over the top about anybody. He could be quite enthusiastic but was never over-enthusiastic. He was never very, very angry – just occasionally a little annoyed. He had such a zest for enjoying life. He just loved life. He loved the simplest possible sorts of things. Most of all, he loved painting. He painted every day, whenever he possibly could. He was always painting.

What he liked about Vanessa was that she was this very maternal figure. He liked thinking of her as though she were a goddess of maternity. She was so beautiful and large and dignified and superb that she looked like a goddess of maternity; she gave that impression; and I think he loved that in her because he felt that she produced a harbour of safety for him, that she'd protect him against anything in the world. Another reason was that she had a great sense of humour and then of course he loved the fact that she was an artist in her own right and understood his painting. They both understood each other's painting and that was a great solace to both of them. It was somehow essential for each of them to be understood by at least one other person in the world, as far as their art went, and they both did that for each other in a wonderful way.

She was madly jealous of his lovers. Duncan's lovers would come to the house and stay, either in Charleston or London, and with some of the men my mother got on extremely well, and loved them. It was when she couldn't find any way of making a relationship with them for herself that she very much resented having them there. And then there was one who was closer to Duncan than the others and she knew this instinctively, and because she was getting older it was very hard for her to put up with.

I love the memories I have of Bloomsbury. I love the people. There are moments that I feel quite nostalgic about the people and I would give anything for the sky to open and some of them to come down and we could all be together, gossiping, laughing together. I would love to have a conversation with Leonard Woolf or someone. I would adore it, because there are so many more things that I could say now than I could say then and I'd love to see how they would react to them, and I'm sure we would clinch even more and it would be wonderful.

Plate 15
CECIL WOOLF

Plate 16
CECIL WOOLF'S HOUSE
Firescreen by Duncan Grant.

CECIL WOOLF

Like his uncle, Leonard Woolf, Cecil Woolf founded his own publishing company, working sometimes, with his wife, Jean, at the same table on which Leonard and Virginia set their hand-operated printing press.

I am, 'the boy with the sloping nose' in Virginia's diaries. I remember Virginia very hazily. I was fourteen when she died. She was immensely lively and gay. She asked one endless questions, and questions followed questions. When you took the train she would want to know not was it a good journey, but everything about the journey: 'What were you reading in the carriage and who else was there? What were they wearing? What were *they* reading?' She wasn't at all fierce, though grown-ups outside her own circle were terrified of her.

If you wanted to see Virginia, you had to get past Leonard. Without Leonard there would have been no Virginia. She needed a great deal of management and Leonard spent his life looking after her. He was obviously very much in love with her. It is hard to understand other people's relationships and I never discussed his marriage with Leonard but I've always been struck by intelligent people's interest in Leonard's and Virginia's sex life, and of course I know nothing about that, nothing that isn't already published. I think it ended in the early 'twenties, because of her frigidity, but I don't think Virginia was a lesbian. There are love letters between Vita and Virginia. They came out in a book twenty years ago that was never published in England. Leonard banned publication. I suppose he felt the time wasn't right for it, that people weren't ready for those kinds of revelations. Today we're much more open-minded. But there's no doubt about their marriage. He was very loving, and it's not everybody who could cope not just with the sexual frigidity, but with the dealing with insanity – suddenly finding out in your early forties that your wife had gone mad.

Everything was very carefully managed by Leonard. I remember Barbara Bagenal saying that one day she was having lunch with them and Virginia suddenly pushed all the food off her plate – I suppose really she was anorexic at times – but she just pushed all the food off her plate onto the table and Leonard took her by the arm and led her to her bedroom and put her in bed. He knew that this was a sign, that it was the beginning of a nervous breakdown. Virginia needed to maintain about nine and a half stones. If she went below that, she started to have a breakdown.

Leonard started the press when he felt he couldn't succeed as a writer. He had always been interested in publishing and printing but when they decided they would go to school to learn how to print they found out they were too old to be accepted: Leonard was thirty-seven; Virginia was thirty-five. And they were told they had to have a union ticket to be a printer. They felt bitterly disappointed about this but then they bought a press and taught themselves. Virginia needed distraction. Although I believe that Leonard himself denied the therapy theory.

Leonard and Virginia set their books from hot metal. Each letter, each space, each comma was an individual entity. There would be a big box of letters divided up into compartments and each compartment would contain lots of little a's, and b's, and so on. It's a little bit like children's printing sets today. That is how printing worked in those days in England. Fifty of their early books were hand-set, mostly by Virginia. A lot of letters are upside down. Leonard did the printing. She set them and he machined them. With a little book, they would do just one page at a time. Virginia would set up a page and he would print twenty copies, say, and then go on to page two, and then page three.

Leonard was a man of very strong views. One of the problems he had as a publisher, and which I share, was not being able to get people. Leonard's staff didn't last. Leonard was a nice man, but very difficult to work for. I remember packing books for him until my hands were sore. The problem was that he expected things to be done his way. He was quite intolerable. There was the feeling that there was no opposing point of view and he was very obstinate. Virginia writes in one of her journals about the car breaking down and Leonard getting out and lifting up the bonnet, rolling up his sleeves and just working and working and working. He refused to be licked. He was a great sticker, my uncle.

Leonard didn't give the appearance of being slightly insecure, but to a younger

Plate 17
MONK'S HOUSE, RODMELL
A bust of Virginia Woolf on the garden wall.

Plate 18
MONK'S HOUSE
A view across the downs from the garden.

Plate 19
MONK'S HOUSE
Virginia Woolf's writing hut is hidden in the foliage.

Plate 20
MONK'S HOUSE
Firescreen, design by Duncan Grant, cross-stitched by Ethel Grant.

generation, that impression seemed clear. His obstinacy was just one manifestation. Another was his carefulness. Leonard and I were at a theatre one evening and sitting next to us was an elderly clergyman who kept rustling the paper from a box of chocolates. During the interval, when the lights went up, the man dropped a chocolate on the floor and I saw Leonard pick it up, get out his handkerchief from his pocket, wipe the chocolate – lovingly, carefully because he was a fastidious man – and pop it in his mouth.

The last day that he was a really well man was a Sunday, June 28th, 1967. His garden was opened to the public once a year, and when the garden closed on this day he was concerned about two girls who had some kind of financial problem. He was eighty-eight, nearly eighty-nine, and was exhausted at the end of a day of being nice to people, shaking hands and so on, and yet he talked for a long time and late into the evening with these two girls and then saw them to the gate. He was a tremendously courteous person. And that was the end, really. That night he had a cerebral hemorrhage and he wandered around the garden all night. The next morning, the gardener came and found him wandering about in the garden in a confused state. Leonard realized he was sick. He was asking for me. I don't want to create the impression that I stayed with him every weekend or was like a son or anything like that. I wasn't. I was a nephew. But it was I he was calling for and I went down. I had a luncheon appointment with Jean and I remember going to pick her up and saying to her, 'Look, Leonard is ill. I've got to go down to Sussex.' Just a few days before, I had seen him running for a bus with a rucksack on his back.

BLOOMSBURY AND CHARLESTON

In 1904 Thoby Stephen was completing his degree at Cambridge University when his father, Sir Leslie Stephen, died after a long illness. This provided an auspicious moment for his children to claim their independence. Thoby would be studying for the Bar when he finished his degree. Adrian would follow his brother's footsteps to Cambridge. But, though they would be accompanied by their brothers, the dramatic move from the traditions of their family home belonged to the two girls. Ignoring advice from elder family members and risking at least some degree of social censure, Vanessa and Virginia availed themselves of the opportunity of their father's

Plate 21
TWILIGHT LANDSCAPE NEAR CHARLESTON

demise to leave his house and set up on their own. That they chose for their new surroundings a decidedly unstylish section of London known as Bloomsbury did not help win them familial approval. But the greater cause for alarm was the fact that though they were not so very young – Vanessa was twenty-five, Virginia, twenty-two – they were unmarried. This, if not a complete breach of mores, was at least cause for severely raised eyebrows among the upper middle-class Victorian social circle in which they had been raised. Undeterred, the two young women further challenged what they considered to be outmoded and stifling prudery by joining their eldest brother, unchaperoned, in late night discussions with his Cambridge friends. With Thoby at Cambridge were Leonard Woolf, Lytton Strachey, Clive Bell, and later, Maynard Keynes. Desmond MacCarthy, who would become London's leading literary and theatre critic, had already taken his degree, but was taking another and had kept his ties with the Apostles, the exclusive and secret society of intellectuals to which they all belonged. Roger Fry, at Cambridge giving lectures on art, became associated through the Apostles and his lectures with Thoby and his friends. These six, with the addition of Lytton's cousin Duncan Grant and Thoby's sisters, became Bloomsbury.

Plate 22
THE STUDIO MANTELPIECE, CHARLESTON

Plate 23
THE STUDIO
Cupboard by Duncan Grant.

It was shortly after Thoby left Cambridge that he established a Thursday get-together to maintain the ties he and his friends had formed at college. The sisters were intrigued and stimulated by the conversation of these young men and gradually joined in their discussions, becoming more and more confident and intimate. Only months after Thoby died of typhoid fever in 1906, Vanessa became engaged to Clive Bell, marrying him in 1907. After shunning an embarrassed and gratefully refused proposal from Lytton Strachey, Virginia married Leonard Woolf in 1912 when he returned from India where he had been a colonial administrator in the British civil service. With their marriages, the two young women became linked to the Cambridge friends permanently.

Leonard became an editor, a writer of columns, reviews and political essays for weekly magazines, a novelist, a biographer. He was the author of twenty books, most of them on politics. He was a staunch socialist and active in the Labour Party, serving for thirty years as secretary of two advisory committees to the government. It was his idea to found the League of Nations, a concept produced following the Great War as preventative against future wars. As the publisher, with Virginia, of the Hogarth Press, he introduced new and experimental writers to the British

Plate 24
VANESSA BELL'S BEDROOM
Cupboard by Vanessa Bell, pastel of Angelica by Duncan Grant.

Plate 25
VANESSA BELL'S BEDROOM
Bust of Angelica by Quentin Bell and oils of Julian by Vanessa Bell.

Plate 26
CLIVE BELL'S STUDY
Fireplace by Vanessa Bell, pottery by Quentin Bell.

Plate 27
THE GARDEN ROOM
Screen by Duncan Grant, cushion design by Vanessa Bell.

Plate 28
CLIVE BELL'S STUDY
Door panels and chair fabric design by Duncan Grant.

public. He was the first to publish Freud in English and it was he who first published T. S. Eliot's epochal poem, *The Waste Land*.

In 1919 John Maynard Keynes published *The Economic Consequences of the Peace*. The book criticized the Allies' severity in the matter of German reparations following World War I, and was written upon Keynes' return from the peace negotiations for which he served as an official of the British Treasury. The outbreak of World War II eventually affirmed his foresight, but the brilliant young author of the book had already gained, with its publication, immediate and international renown. Keynes went on to play a major role in British economic strategy during World War II, make his personal fortune, support the arts and further develop and preach the new branch of economic theory that made him the most influential world figure in that science since Adam Smith.

Giles Lytton Strachey changed the art of biography forever when his debunkings of long-revered Victorian icons was published in 1918. *Eminent Victorians* was an immediate success. Instead of giving a cold, unbiased, reverential account of the incidents of life, Strachey infused his biographies with his own sharp interpretations and psychoanalyses. Clever, lively, irreverent and highly stylistic, the results were

Plate 29
THE STUDIO

Plate 30
THE STUDIO
Cast of the ears of Michelangelo's David.

both scholarly and entertaining. He was interested in motives and feelings, in the person behind and beneath the veneer of the cold hard facts of which most biographies were made and he exposed, often for the first time, the personal and moral shortcomings of his subjects. He followed his early triumph with biographies of Queen Victoria in 1921 and in 1928 of Elizabeth and Essex.

In the autumn of 1910, the first Post-Impressionist exhibition was held in London. It was organized by Roger Fry, a curator recently returned to England from New York's Metropolitan Museum. Meeting Clive and Vanessa Bell on a train, Fry quickly gathered their support for the radical Cézannes and Van Goghs he would be showing and they, in return, enlisted the help of their friends. Clive helped to collect pictures and, as an art critic enthused by the new style of painting, wrote favourably of the ill-received show. Desmond MacCarthy served as secretary and wrote the introduction to the catalogue. When Fry held a second exhibition two years later, Leonard Woolf was secretary. The Bloomsbury artists, Vanessa Bell and Duncan Grant, were influenced by that style for the whole of their lives.

Fry was an appealing lecturer and writer. He addressed art appreciation in layman's terms and in a style of questioning of which Moore would have approved:

Plate 31
DUNCAN GRANT'S DRESSING ROOM
Table by Duncan Grant.

What do we see when we look at a picture? How does an artist arouse our emotions? He believed that the expressions of emotions were ends in themselves and that forms were the crucial evocative elements in a visual work – form followed function. Clive Bell shared those views and in 1914, on Fry's recommendation, published *Art*, in which he introduced the term 'significant form' in support of the theory that colour, line, form and their relationship to one another create the aesthetic experience in a painting and that no exterior knowledge, which only filled the viewer's mind with distracting irrelevancies, was needed. *Art* was a popular book, and Bell followed it some years later with another, *Civilization*.

In 1913, with Duncan Grant as co-director, Fry founded an artists' co-operative, the Omega Workshops, where he put into practice another of his theories – that even commonplace objects should be visually pleasing. Plates, curtains, wallpaper, flowerpots and other items of everyday utility were created by artists who shared his views with the idea that the purpose of objects is to be aesthetically considered and enjoyed. The Omega Workshops closed in 1920, but its lesson was put into full and permanent expression at Charleston, the country home of Clive and Vanessa Bell which they shared with Duncan Grant. In their search for a country house, Clive

Plate 32
CLIVE BELL'S BEDROOM
Bed painted by Vanessa Bell.

Plate 33
THE GARDEN AND HOUSE

Plate 34
THE SPARE BEDROOM
Window surround by Vanessa Bell, terracotta bust by Quentin Bell.

and Vanessa Bell had looked for a farm. It was then wartime. Both Duncan Grant and Bunny Garnett could avoid military service if they found alternative work as farm labourers. Their being pacifists made this type of exemption an attractive alternative to other efforts to keep out of the war; Lytton Strachey had taken his case to the courts, winning his own exemption by declaring, to the embarrassment of the court and the amusement of the crowd who had packed in to witness the trial, his own homosexuality. Virginia and Leonard were renting a house about four miles from Charleston, so Vanessa knew the South Downs well. It was Virginia who encouraged her sister to look into Charleston.

Clive, Vanessa and Duncan all lived in Charleston until their deaths. Vanessa in 1961, Clive in 1964, Duncan in 1978, when he was 93. Though the Bells always kept rooms in London, which Clive in particular was in the habit of using, leaving Charleston to the painters, Charleston was their principal residence from the war onwards. Charleston Farmhouse, sometimes called 'Bloomsbury by the sea', was where Bloomsbury gathered for weekends and dinner parties and the house was regularly full of friends and visitors: Leonard and Virginia, Lytton, Desmond MacCarthy, Roger Fry, T. S. Eliot, G. E. Moore, Bertrand Russell, E. M. Forster,

Plate 35
THE GARDEN
The orchard and cast of the Venus de Milo.

Kenneth Clark, Benjamin Britten, Raymond Mortimer. It was where Maynard Keynes wrote *The Economic Consequences of the Peace*. In later years, it was mostly painters who came, and mostly Duncan they came to see. However, Duncan and Vanessa had a rare artistic compatability, were lifelong friends and working companions. Charleston, hand-painted from floor to ceiling, was their most complex aesthetic collaboration.

But perhaps Virginia Woolf's name shines with the greatest brightness. By the time she died, in 1941, she had written seventeen books. With her physical frailty, mental instability, intellectual independence, sharp tongue, great beauty and suicide, she has emerged as a tragic figure. But her position, gained early in her career, as one of the key writers at the forefront of the modern psychological novel has earned her an unassailable position in English literary history; her novels are still read, her hundreds of essays still regularly considered to be unsurpassed.

Bloomsbury existed during a volatile time of intellectual tumult and technological change. The strict moral code of the Victorians was exposed as hypocrisy and replaced with candour and freedom; a world of peace and prosperity was twice shattered by world war and, as the twentieth century unfolded into the global age, Bloomsbury added their own voices to the clamour of modernism.

Plate 36
ST. MICHAEL AND ALL ANGELS CHURCH, BERWICK
Berwick Church lies just three miles from Charleston Farmhouse.
During the war Duncan Grant and Vanessa Bell decorated the interior of
the church. The models for the scenes portrayed on the walls were friends, relatives and
local people and were originally painted wearing boiler suits, but such was the parish
outcry that Duncan had to repaint them in robes of religious tradition.
'The Nativity' by Vanessa Bell.

Plate 37
BERWICK CHURCH
Altar screen roundels of the seasons by Duncan Grant.

Plate 38
BERWICK CHURCH
The pulpit by Duncan Grant.

HUGH CECIL

Hugh Cecil is the second of Desmond and Molly MacCarthy's grandchildren by their daughter, Rachel, and the writer Lord David Cecil. Hugh, a professor of modern English history at Leeds University, lives in London and with his wife, Mirabel, has recently written his grandfather's biography.

If you wanted an advertisement for not smoking, it was Desmond. He had appalling lung trouble. I think he'd had a very good physique when he was young – he'd always run for buses and all of that. He hated not being able to burn the candle at both ends, but of course it was the result of doing that, really, that was the end of him. He wrote up until the day he died. Though he was in very bad shape physically, his mind was perfect. There was no reason why he should have stopped working. His mind was absolutely as vigorous as ever. The mind sort of filled the house, as well as the body. When you went into the hall, if he was ill, you'd hear him wheezing in his bedroom. He kept the door open and the maid – he had a rather slightly disagreeable but kindly maid – would rush in and dispense whatever had to be dispensed to an asthma patient. So you always heard this awful wheezing sound. But when he was well and up and about, then the house was filled with his lively, jovial presence. He laughed a great deal, with a good deal of wheezing, it is true, but he did laugh a lot. He liked being amused.

Though my grandfather wasn't absolutely a member of Bloomsbury, he is perhaps most frequently thought of as a member of Bloomsbury. That, in a way, is how his name has survived. There are lots of literary figures who are of the same eminence as Desmond MacCarthy who have faded away from memory. I think Bloomsbury and the interest in it, the cult, if you like, has rather helped a lot of people.

He was less sexually experimental than others in the Bloomsbury world. He was

Plate 39
HUGH CECIL, DESMOND MACCARTHY
AND JONATHAN CECIL
with a portrait of their grandfather.

only a few years older, but I think it made a difference. He was very conservative, morally. In a way, he was pretty innocent, and I think he rather regretted it, actually. I think he rather envied the others their sexual freedoms. He was very fond of ladies. He got on frightfully well with them, and he did use to go to a lot of places without Molly, partly because she was very deaf and partly because she didn't like going to London, but he wasn't a lady killer.

I think you'd learn something very significant about the times from studying Bloomsbury. They were very original, but they were typical of a particular upper middle-class type of society of that period in that they had a certain amount of money which enabled them to live a very agreeable life – a highly civilized, cultivated life which seems to be particular to that time as opposed to this one. They were wonderfully secure, although that wasn't quite true of Desmond. Some of them were quite rich – Keynes, in particular – but generally they had financial security without being rich people. They had an extraordinarily privileged life, in a way. They belonged to the right side of society, in terms of advantage, in a period when the advantaged side of society had it very good, indeed. They had servants, for instance, which made it easier for them to lead a very interesting, very cultivated way of life. They could cultivate their minds and their friendships. It was in the best sense a life of leisure, which is not to say that they were idle. Virginia and Leonard Woolf were constantly working, as was Roger Fry. They had a sort of Aristotelian sense of leisure, which does not seem possible now.

Plate 40
HUGH CECIL

JONATHAN CECIL

The eldest son of Desmond and Molly MacCarthy's first child, Rachel, Jonathan Cecil remembers his grandfather with a lucid clarity. He is an actor, as was for a time his mother.

He really was the most wonderful man. He had a gift, which very few people have, of radiating a kind of sympathetic and cheerful atmosphere so that he made everybody in the room feel as though what they had to say was important, even a small boy, as I was. Everything was taken seriously as a perfectly fair comment and interesting. 'Why did you say that?' he would say, and 'Oh, how interesting'. He was a wonderful talker, but everybody says that. But he was a wonderful bringer-out of other people. The people who get along best with children tend to be people who treat the child as if he were their own age, or a grown-up person. He never patronized me.

I can remember his library in Garrick's Villa, the country house of the famous actor David Garrick which had been turned into rather superior flats and where he used to live, he and my grandmother, in their final years. I can remember talking to him there. I call it his library because it was more like a library than a study because it was piled high with books. I can see it now. There was a bust of him by someone, and a bust of Julius Caesar. And he would be in there, writing. It would be in the evening, after tea time. In England, tea time doesn't exist now, except in the smart hotels. Until the end of their lives my parents used to have a set tea at five o'clock in the evening, with tea and sandwiches and cake. I don't think people do it anymore; we certainly don't. But we did then, and after tea, my grandfather would ask me to come up and talk to him in the library. I would sit down in the armchair opposite and I remember this overpowering smell of tobacco, which now as a reformed smoker I find repellent, but then nobody did because it was all over the place and there was something rather reassuring I thought about a room which was impregnated with pipe smoke. It had a sort of old-fashioned feel. So I would sit there and I would ask him questions – I'd just begun to see Shakespeare's plays – and he would answer to the best of his ability.

It is impossible to describe the sort of exuberance my grandfather had. He had a tremendous zest for life, and he liked silly jokes. One time, when I was around eleven or twelve, my mother and I went Christmas shopping just outside London, near Hampton Court, where my grandparents lived. We bought various things for Christmas and I bought some things I thought could be useful in a show I was putting on with my friends. One of these props was a fake banana: a rubber banana which squeaked. When we got home, my mother put it on the table among all the real bananas and the other fruit and said to him, when he came in, 'Daddy, you must have this banana'. He said, 'Oh, I don't think it looks very ripe'. But he finally picked it up and finding that it was fake and that it squeaked, well, he thought that was most amusing. We were delighted with this. But he loved all that. I remember my mother telling me that when they were children and getting into a train, he always used to say, as the train was leaving, 'And off went the jolly MacCarthys'.

Milo Keynes got to know the Bloomsbury Group through his uncle, Maynard Keynes, and Maynard's wife, Lydia Lopokova, whom Maynard met when she was dancing with the Russian Ballet. Milo is a physician in Cambridge.

Maynard was the centre of Bloomsbury. He was such a leading figure all around that he was bound to be the centre. When Maynard left Cambridge to go into the civil service, he moved in to share houses with them in Gordon Square. There, he wrote a thesis for Cambridge and was writing political works and was very involved with a journal called *The Nation*, which later merged with *The New Statesman*. He was concerned with getting the editor to write what he thought ought to be written.

He was very quick-thinking. He used to tackle problems and then he could change his mind to other problems very quickly, so that the amount of work he did in any given day was truly amazing. He could shift his thoughts so he could give half an hour at the beginning of the day to the stock exchange and making himself money to keep going, and then he might be writing about economics, or giving reports to the Treasury or planning what the publications he was interested in should be producing, criticising and writing about people. There are thirty volumes of his collected writings. And then he had to keep Lydia amused and going, and do the artistic side of his life. He had a large picture collection, which he donated to the Fitzwilliam Museum in Cambridge. He started the Arts Theatre in Cambridge. He built it entirely with his own money, and then donated it. The idea was that it would be somewhere for Lydia Lopokova to perform, not as a dancer but as an actress, and she did. He also financed the Camargo Society, which began putting on ballets after Diaghilev was gone and became, in effect, the Royal Ballet. And he was lecturing and teaching at Cambridge and running the finances of King's. He had an immense psychic energy which allowed him to develop all of his great endowment. He was a fabulous man.

Plate 41
MILO KEYNES

ANN SYNGE

Virginia Woolf's niece, Ann Synge, was just two years old when she moved to 50 Gordon Square with her parents, Adrian and Karen Stephen. She lived there until her university years, and then again in the 1930s. Clive Bell lived upstairs, on the top two floors. Virginia and Leonard lived nearby, in Tavistock Square. Maynard Keynes lived a few houses away, as did Lytton Strachey's brother, James, and his wife, Alix. James and Alix were psychoanalysts – James translated the works of Sigmund Freud for the Woolfs' Hogarth Press – as were Synge's parents. They had all gone to Vienna to be psychoanalyzed by Dr. Freud, returning to London, to Bloomsbury, to set up practices of their own.

I knew they weren't ordinary people, everyone was always saying about them, 'So distinguished, so remarkable'. My parents were always busy with travelling and with patients, so I saw Bloomsbury mostly through the eyes of the servants. 'Pretty odd', they would say, 'but geniuses'. It was a remarkable childhood, but I wasn't aware of it at the time. I thought everyone's house was like this. I had talents to be a psychoanalyst, but when I saw how peculiar my parents were, I didn't go into it.

We were the outsiders of the family. My father a little bit resented being always referred to as my aunt's brother. He resented all the attention over Bloomsbury. He didn't court publicity, but wouldn't have minded being part of the group. And I always was very envious of Vanessa's children because they got all the attention. Virginia was everybody's favourite. It was, 'Oh, Virginia's coming to tea! Hurrah! Hurrah! Have a good time!'

Plate 42
ANN SYNGE

ANTHONY FRY

Like many of the Bloomsbury descendants, Anthony Fry followed in his family's footsteps. His second cousin, the painter, curator, and teacher, Roger Fry, provided the influence that led him to become a painter.

Roger always thought of himself as a painter, but he was a terrible painter. I hated his paintings. We in the family thought they were ghastly. But he was an electrifying speaker. He would bring people to tears. He talked about painting as no critic has before or since. He talked about it in a physical way – the paint, the transparency of paint. It was infinitely more interesting than the normal way. With his lectures, he led people toward the avant-garde. It was he who invented the term 'Post-Impressionist'.

I was very influenced by the ideas he put forward with the Omega, the idea of covering a surface with art, with not obeying the constraints of a conventional surface, but allowing the art to dominate. In painting a cupboard, for instance, the design would go past the shelves onto the wall to which the cupboard was attached. Or the design could travel down the leg of a table, rather than being stopped at the table's edge. It was a question of freedom. Art was not precious. I grew up eating off the tables, the china, the pottery. The Omega was really the most important aspect of Bloomsbury. It is only recently that a new surge of interest has grown up around them, and while the paintings may not last, their influence will.

Bloomsbury were regarded with derision when I grew up. They were elitist, snobby and by being so frightened a lot of people off. Roger's sister Marjorie always said that she would never go to Bloomsbury meetings. They were too cold. They didn't welcome one. There were, she said, horrific, high-powered, intellectual sparrings and they were extremely alarming for an outsider. As people, they don't come out in a saintly way. They were too insular. They did not embrace new ideas.

Plate 43
ANTHONY FRY

My father and Roger were very good friends. Roger was always telling my father what to do with what pictures he had. He was a very strong influence in my father's life because he took such an interest in everything my father was doing. I never made a conscious decision to be a painter. I never had the slightest doubt, from the age of eight, that that was what I was going to do. That whole atmosphere was my background. It was my world – the atmosphere they gave off. I was always surrounded by pictures by Roger Fry and Duncan Grant. All these heroic lives. I was surrounded by them.

Plate 44
SISSINGHURST CASTLE, KENT
Vita Sackville-West's garden.

NIGEL NICOLSON

The son of writer Vita Sackville-West and diplomat Harold Nicolson, Nigel Nicolson, a writer, editor, publisher, and one-time member of Parliament, lives at Sissinghurst, the family mansion famed for the gardens designed by his parents.

It was a strange life: my brother, Ben, and I in one building, our parents in another, Vita in the Tower, and all of us running around in the rain. We hardly knew anybody around here. The sort of people who would come for dinner parties were younger politicians like Harold Macmillan – my father's friends – and there would be literary people like Cyril Connolly. It was almost a Bloomsbury in the country, except that no one ever stayed. We had no guest rooms. My mother always said that if you had guest rooms you were likely to have guests!

My parents' parties were more fun than Bloomsbury parties, I think, because in Bloomsbury there was always an element of competition and of being on trial and mostly it was the central seven who were the ringmasters. Bloomsbury was a frightening place. The first time I attended a Bloomsbury party I just sat there trying to hide. Vita was scared, too. She always called them, 'Gloomsbury'. Vanessa didn't like her and would say so in her presence. Virginia admired Vanessa's acerbity. A lot of the Bloomsbury malice was a product of their love of wit and the fact that they were very competitive. In Charleston they were much softer and so it was less intimidating than London Bloomsbury. There was more time and fewer people and so they were less sharp. In London, when they had to do everything in just a couple of hours, they were much more biting and quick. At Charleston, they had all weekend, so it stretched out and was softer.

It could be very alarming entering a Bloomsbury party. I remember one – there were about ten or eleven people there and I and my mother were there. I was about sixteen years old. Virginia told one of her stories. She could be very funny and this was a particularly amusing story and everybody laughed. Then she turned to the youngest person in the room – apart from myself; they were kind to people my age – and said to the young woman, 'Now you tell us a story'. Of course it was supremely

Plate 45
NIGEL NICOLSON

unkind and the girl burst into tears. But it was Bloomsbury's way of saying, 'Now see here, if you want to join in our parties and become a member of the group, you've got to make a contribution; otherwise, we're not interested'. Once that happened to you and you failed the test, then they didn't want you to come back and you didn't want to go back. So it did become rather an exclusive group.

But in spite of their intellectual superiority, I must give them credit for having succeeded in one of the most difficult things anybody can attempt, which is to give an art a new form which will be convincing to their contemporaries and influential for at least two generations to come. And they did this not only in one art line, like the Pre-Raphaelites did, but in a whole range of things: fiction, obviously, and art criticism, literary criticism, paintings, economics. They did really cover a very wide span. And in each of these arts the Bloomsbury figure who was central to it made this enduring innovation and contribution which is still influential to us. It affects our lives in ways we don't even realize. And their social attitudes had an influence. At the time, social life was reeking with all sorts of conventions from the Victorian Age and Bloomsbury freed us from those. They established patterns from which we are still the beneficiaries – our liberal attitude toward marriage, for instance. They were unfaithful to each other but their infidelities tended to be permanent. Like Vanessa and Duncan.

I've always been surprised by how easily Virginia slipped into her love affair with my mother, because Virginia never in her life experienced such a thing before, and she was nearly thirty years old when it began. Vita was ten years younger. When Virginia was a young woman, little more than a teenager, she had herself a flirtatious relationship with another girl, Violet Dickinson. It never led to anything more than an exchange of sort of schoolgirl pleasantries. And in her later life she met Ethel Smythe, but that was obviously nothing like the physical relationship she had with Vita. So the Vita affair was Virginia's only love affair. In her marriage, you see, she had been sexually and totally frigid. I don't think she and Leonard went to bed together but once or twice. And that's why it surprises me so much that Virginia entered into this affair.

Plate 46
VITA SACKVILLE-WEST'S DESK

Plate 47
ADAM NICOLSON WITH HIS SON

I think it was actually she who seduced Vita. I don't think it was the other way around because Vita, who had had plenty of lesbian love affairs, was too frightened of precipitating a new attack of madness in Virginia. She knew that Virginia was totally inexperienced sexually and thought that to expose her to actual physical love might trigger a new attack of lunacy. My father actually warned her about it in a letter. He was staying in Prussia. He and Vita corresponded daily. Of course, the letters took six weeks to arrive, but even so, Vita confessed what was happening and he wrote back, saying, 'Fine, but I worry about the harm you might do to Virginia, who's balanced on a knife edge, mentally'. I mean, Virginia adored her and they had a delicious time for about three years, beginning in 1925, or so. All their friends knew about it. Of course, Bloomsbury didn't discuss these things openly. They would talk to the people concerned about it. They would talk to each other absolutely without any sense of shock.

On two occasions Vanessa and Vita came close to each other, or closer. The first was when Vanessa's son Julian was killed in the Spanish Civil War. Vita wrote a letter of sympathy to Vanessa, not really expecting an answer. But Vanessa replied, thanking her for it and saying, 'You can't think what a help Virginia has been to me all this time. Without her, I don't think I would have survived, but I can't bring myself to tell her, my being her older sister, what I owed to her and my gratitude, so would you tell her what I feel?' And Vita, of course, did tell Virginia. It was so dramatic in the relationship between the two sisters, that although they were so close, they couldn't express to each other their most profound emotions. And it also illustrates the attitude of Vanessa towards my mother. She couldn't help but love her because she shared Virginia with her. I mean, they were the two women together who meant the most to Virginia Woolf.

The other time that Vanessa and Vita came together was when Virginia killed herself and Vanessa asked Vita to come and see her at Charleston. I think it was only the second time that Vita had ever been to Charleston. Of course she went, and the two women spent two hours together talking, obviously, about Virginia. No record, of course, of their conversation survives, but there were letters written both before and after they met which were suddenly so intimate, and I have those letters here. They have not been published, but one day they should be. So that was the second occasion. After that, for the rest of their lives, I don't think Vanessa and Vita ever met again. But it ended on that note. This sudden intimacy when they were brought together by the death or the suicide of the woman who was close to both of them.

The affair between Vita and Virginia had no effect at all on their marriages. The husbands knew all about it. They were, in a sense, delighted. I know my father was. I'm not so sure Leonard was, because he cared for Virginia's mental health, as well. But when Vita and Virginia decided to go away together to France on holiday in 1928, there were no protests from the husbands. Their marriages, of course, were very much alike. One difference was that Leonard was not gay, and my father was. But Leonard wasn't and as far as I know Leonard never betrayed Virginia, even when she went with another woman. My father didn't have the same view. He'd have his men friends. But in other ways, they were very similar – in the sense that they were people with independent careers and they were deeply and immensely devoted to their spouses. Leonard deliberately gave up his career in the colonial service to marry Virginia. He waited until she agreed to marry him before he sent in his resignation. And it was my father who had saved my parents' marriage, when Vita was going to leave him, not long after they had married, for Violet Trefusis. So there was no indication of a breakup of their marriages. All four of them had independent reputations and social lives. They gave each other liberty, and each encouraged the other to produce the best of which each was capable.

There is no more Bloomsbury. We have no contact with one another, except when we meet to lecture at a symposium. I met Quentin as a child, but I have never really known him well. The children are not a Bloomsbury circle or even a continuation of the circle. We have not carried on the ideas of our parents. We are not like them though we are writers and painters and that sort of thing. They never added young people, except for their children. Many never had children. They didn't have any successors, either. They didn't hand on the cultural torch to another group. They were unique and now they are dropping like apples in the autumn.

ADAM NICOLSON

Adam Nicolson is the second of Nigel Nicolson's three children and the only son. A writer, Adam lives in a sprawling town house in Cambridge with his wife, Olivia, and their three young sons.

The thing about Cambridge is that everyone feels that they don't really belong when they're at Cambridge. Everyone says, 'I'm a misfit here'. Most people feel gawky and the Apostles are a sort of self-selecting elite of people who feel above it all, sort of removed. Even the name Apostles has a sort of purity. It's very, very Cambridge, that: sort of cut-off. They think that they are such extraordinary misfits, that they're vastly superior. But that doesn't really fit, to me, to that whole philosophy of G. E. Moore – this idea of selected friendships. The whole Bloomsbury thing is highly selective. It's a brutal kind of culture. The Apostles still exist, but it's secret. It's an establishment that really works on knowing secrets. It's not about conspicuous display at all. It's very classy to be an Apostle, still. I wasn't one. I wasn't clever enough. You have to be very, very clever.

It seems to me that in the 'olden days' it was much easier for people like Keynes to be an art collector and interested in art and be friends with artists, or, say, for Harold to be both a diplomat and a writer and a critic and so on. There was more coherence between the worlds of art and diplomacy and politics than there is now. When you think of a politician now, it's a sterilized picture you have of this blathering career man. Maybe it was easier then for a group of friends who might do various things to actually integrate with each other.

I'm really shackled by ignorance, but I don't know how much of this whole idea of their being a group is really fiction, whether they were, in fact, this homogenous gang. It seems that the relationship to the group of Hadji (Harold) and Vita was like a string off the edge, and that leads one to think Bloomsbury wasn't this sort of little tight thing. Obviously, it's in the nature of friendships that there are strings going out all the time. There was a sort of group philosophy about friendship and conversation and so on. It wasn't just a gang of friends who happened to do well in different fields.

REMINISCENCES

FRANCES PARTRIDGE

When Frances Marshall met Ralph Partridge she was just out of university and working in a London book store. Ralph was working for the Hogarth Press. He was living outside London with Lytton Strachey and Dora Carrington. Carrington and Lytton had become inseparable some years before – though he was homosexual, Lytton was to remain the great passion of Carrington's life – and when Ralph met them, introduced by Carrington's brother Noel, a friend and fellow rower of Ralph's at Oxford, he fell in love with her. Lytton was also extremely fond of Ralph and when, in 1921, Ralph and Carrington married, Ralph agreed to maintain the household his wife and Lytton had set up at Tidmarsh. Within a few months of her marriage, Carrington had a love affair with another of Ralph's friends, the writer Gerald Brenan. If the result of this was to shatter Ralph's marital feelings for Carrington and free him emotionally so that he could fall in love with Frances, it did nothing to disrupt the strange ménage at Tidmarsh. In 1924, Ralph and Lytton purchased Ham Spray, a country house in Wiltshire, not far from the Tidmarsh home. The following year, with Ralph's relationship with Frances intensifying, Lytton made clear what his response would be if Ralph were to separate from Carrington: he would leave both Carrington and Ham Spray. When it became clear to all how possibly mortally devastating this would be to Carrington, Frances and Ralph agreed that Ralph should continue to maintain not only his marriage but also his life at Ham Spray. They would live together in London during the week and Ralph would spend his weekends and holidays with Lytton and Carrington.

In 1926, Frances and Ralph moved into Gordon Square together. Lytton rented the rooms below theirs to use when he needed to spend time in London. They continued in this fashion until Lytton's death, in 1932, and Carrington's grief-driven suicide seven weeks later. Ralph and Frances married the following year and moved into Ham Spray, where they wrote – Ralph was a book binder and a literary critic – and raised their only child, Lytton Burgo Partridge, who died in 1963 at the age of twenty-eight. He had married Henrietta Garnett just months before.

When Ralph died, in 1960, Frances sold the house and moved to London. In addition to two popular Bloomsbury memoirs and two volumes of diaries, her literary career has included editing The Greville Memoirs with Ralph, compiling the index for Leonard's English edition of the works of Sigmund Freud and translating French and Spanish literature. Continuing to mine the Bloomsbury vein, she also published A Bloomsbury Album, a collection of snapshots of her friends and family through the Bloomsbury years, and she wrote the introduction to a reissue of Lytton Strachey's Eminent Victorians. Hard into her eighties, she still practices the violin and continues her lifelong habit of keeping a journal, filling spiral composition notebooks with her neat, tight script.

As soon as I'd *really* met them – and I was only twenty-two and fairly unconfident – I thought, '*these* are the people I want to see and know. They're far more interesting and alive and full of ideas and not just sort of sticking to the rules.'

I was living with my mother in another Bloomsbury square, but there were lots of Bloomsbury parties. That was a great feature of life. They weren't sort of very alchoholic parties, but there was lots of dancing, and Rafe was a very keen dancer and so was I and we got together from these parties. I was fascinated by his vitality and unconventionality and his gift for communication. Then I was invited down to stay where he was living at Tidmarsh with Lytton and Carrington, and they'd already had some trouble, he and Carrington, about Gerald Brenan, who was his best friend.

Everybody was rather carrying on freely and he rather made up to me and I didn't quite know what to make of it all. And then, I can't say, it's very difficult to say when you fall in love with somebody, but I don't think it was until 1925, when Rafe persuaded me to go to Spain with him, and we did go and when we came back we decided that we would try and live together and make it a joint ménage. It was then that we looked for somewhere to live and found somewhere right in Gordon Square in the house of James Strachey, Lytton's brother, and Alix.

All this was done with a lot of – not without a certain pain and anguish – but no loss of friendship. That is, we went down weekends to Ham Spray often, and sometimes Rafe would perhaps go off for a holiday with Lytton and Carrington. The whole problem was complicated by the fact that the man Carrington adored was Lytton and she was terrified of losing Lytton, rather than of losing Rafe. She was very fond of Rafe, and relied on him because he was very sort of a reliable character. They both did. He and Lytton were

devoted friends, and though his marriage to Carrington had come to grief within two years, they remained close friends, as they did with Lytton. It turned out all right. It had ups and downs and persisted until they died. When Lytton was ill it was a time of very great crisis. Everybody was very agitated, because he was very young. He was fifty-one when he died. He was very young, though he didn't seem so, then, to many of us.

Everybody was very civilized. Bloomsbury ethics, after all, were not conventional. They never thought about what the world thought, or of convention. I came from a more conventional background. In a sense my family were all liberal and that, but for me to go and what's called 'live in sin', was rather a step, really. They'd hoped I'd do a little better than that. They liked Rafe, or, rather, my mother did. My father had been dead for several years. It worked out all right, and amicably.

I believed in human happiness, and I was very much a pacifist. I was a pacifist when I was sixteen years old. I hated violence. I was certainly left wing. I hate inequality. Bunny – and I won't say a word against him – when you talked about egalitarianism with him in his later years he would turn very pink in the face. I see nothing wrong with it. I think everyone should have an equal chance, and that is just the result of my own thinking.

I think the odd thing about Bloomsbury is that so many of them lived in one square, in Gordon Square. It was like living at Cambridge. One side of Gordon Square was all filled with Bloomsbury people. There was somebody in every single building. As time went on and the Bloomsbury Group went down in the generations and they had more friends on the outside, they were still deeply attached, and we had a link which was a thing called the Memoir Club. The occasions of its meetings were delightful. We had dinner together and after would have the reading of, say, two papers, which were very enjoyable, generally, and there would be discussion and wine drinking and a jolly evening. It was a chance, at a time when everybody had split up and married and lived far away or gone to work to some university, to collect. It was a focal point for all those people who weren't close together at Charleston and Rodmell. But it was possibly too exclusive. We all sort of came from the same families, in the end. Some of us wanted outside blood, but there was a system of blackballing, which meant that others couldn't get in.

I was sort of between generations, between the major people – Vanessa and Clive – and the Quentin generation. When Quentin and Julian and Angelica were growing up, they were all friends who continued to visit us and then married into our family and it all became very complicated. I think the family tree of the Garnetts and the Partridges must be impossible because of Bunny's first wife being my sister! So that though Burgo and Henrietta seemed to be cousins; and were both related to Bunny – Burgo by marriage to Henrietta – they were two sorts of relations at once and had no blood in common, it's very confusing. I don't recommend trying to understand it.

GEORGE RYLANDS

When George Rylands entered Cambridge, he embarked on an academic career that was to last his lifetime. The rooms into which he moved as a young don, in 1927, when he was twenty-five years old, are the same rooms he occupies today, its doors and walls painted, in true Bloomsbury style, by his friends Dora Carrington and Douglas Davidson, and his cupboards filled and tables covered with collections of china – entire dinner services – and Victorian children's books. In his study, where he writes on an old manual typewriter, he keeps the rare Shakespeare folios he will bequeath to the college at his death. But his legacy at Cambridge has been of far greater value than the books he collected.

By the time he retired from teaching, in 1967, Rylands had recorded the entire works of Shakespeare for the British Broadcasting Company, trained directors and actors – Peter Hall, Trevor Nunn, John Gielgud and Ian McKellen among them – in Shakespeare's diction, and acted in or directed every major Shakespeare play. This was in addition to his teaching, lecturing and writing. In the 1930s he was Maynard Keynes' right-hand man when Keynes decided to build, with his own money, a theatre for Cambridge.

Like his contemporary and fellow Cambridge undergraduate Frances Partridge, Rylands is some twenty years younger than the central, founding members of the Bloomsbury Group. But Bloomsbury was never so elitist as to exclude younger acquaintances from their circle and Rylands was friends with many of them. He was, in fact, one of the few who survived mention in Virginia Woolf's critical and caustic diaries without a slashing critique. 'Indeed for Dadie', she wrote, referring to him by the nickname by which he was, and continues to be, known to all close to him, 'I feel considerable affection. So sensitive and tender is he'.

It was after the deaths of Lytton and Virginia that people began to get interested in Bloomsbury. Keynes was world-famous as an economist, and Duncan's and Vanessa's paintings were beginning to be known, but when Lytton and Virginia died, people were suddenly aware that two remarkable people who had done remarkable things had gone. It was just before and just after the second world war that Bloomsbury became an entity, though it had been growing in that direction since the 1930s. When all the books started coming out about them, I didn't get involved. I thought it was very tiresome. I have very vivid memories and emotions and feelings about all the people who were good to me – Lytton and Carrington, Maynard and Lydia, Leonard and Virginia – and much of what was said was untrue and I didn't want to hear of it. Extraordinary myths about Bloomsbury were propounded. People had their own ideas and theories and they like to get them out. But things got all distorted.

When I came down from Cambridge in 1924, I had already met Leonard and Virginia when I stayed the previous year in a house in Dorset which Maynard Keynes and Lydia had rented for a summer holiday. They asked me for a weekend and there I met Raymond Mortimer, who became a lifelong friend (Oxford, of course, but it is very good to have a bit of Oxford put into one's Cambridge veins) and then I met Leonard and Virginia. They knew that I was interested in printing and that I was coming down in a year's time. They had already had several people who were going to go into the Hogarth Press. There was a whole series of persons who went in and didn't last very long. None of us lasted very long. We weren't paid and we weren't happy. Leonard thought we were all incompetent.

Anyway, I said I was looking forward to some kind of future in publishing. They had recently moved from Richmond back to Bloomsbury where I then went and lived in Gordon Square with an undergraduate friend of mine, Douglas Davidson. His brother Angus became, after me, one of the team who failed at the Hogarth Press, ending in a glorious affair with my young friend John Lehmann. But anyway, it was very thrilling. I had hardly ever been to London before, and I arrived and Douglas Davidson and I had two floors on the top of a house which was lived in and rented by Duncan and Vanessa. A little bit up the road were Maynard and Lydia and James and Alix Strachey, who had just come back from studying with Freud in Vienna and who were setting up as psychoanalysts. A little further up the road were Lady Strachey and Pippa and Marjorie. The whole of that side of Gordon Square

was entirely filled with Bloomsburys.

So I went there and shared those rooms and went just around the corner into Tavistock Square – where Leonard and Virginia were living – and into the basement to work at the Hogarth Press. They taught me how you filled out an invoice and how you did up a parcel and how you set up type. For a little while, I set up type with Virginia, but not for very long because she and Leonard then went off to Rodmell, in Sussex, and I was left totally alone with a comical old girl who was doing up parcels in the basement. It was really terrifying. I had also been taught roughly how to work the little tiny press and the big foot press, which the Nicolsons' have got. I was usually totally covered with ink and was perfectly hopeless at it and was absolutely terrified. I was only there about six months, but I became very, very great friends for life after that. Until they both died. They used to come here to see my productions of plays. We became very close friends.

The only bit of printing that I can look back on now, that was of any interest, was that not long after I had been there, a traveller for several booksellers came along, who said, 'We want a copy of *The Wasteland*'. Well, by that time, *The Wasteland* was not being particularly well reviewed. It had not been a large edition and it was more or less out of print. He found ten copies or so on the shelves, but they didn't have any little label saying *The Wasteland* on the outside cover. One of the first and only things I'm proud of having done was that I printed the labels for those.

The other great excitement was a book called *The Rector's Daughter*, which was printed by them. Their niece Tess Rothschild was one of my dearest friends and this was her aunt, and it was a great success and it was the first novel, before Leonard and Virginia published Vita Sackville-West's bestsellers. They had, of course, published *Jacob's Room*, but it hadn't made a great stir. This was a sort of popular old-style Edwardian novel and it had a wonderful success, and it was a brand new event in the Hogarth Press. So they collected all the extracts of the reviews of a favourable kind and I printed a leaflet of those. Very proud of that.

But I couldn't go on with it, partly because I was burning the candle at both ends and London in 1924 and 1925 was pretty glamorous because the war was over and it was thought that there could never be another war and everyone was enjoying themselves. I had never been to London before, and we were asked out by various people. So what with that and the terrible difficulty with one's white evening waistcoat and not getting printer's ink on it and tying one's white tie without getting a smudge was very tricky. Plus, I was writing my dissertation for a fellowship here which was called *Words and Poetry* and which was then published by the Hogarth Press. Half is about the diction of poetry, at that moment I thought I had ideas which had been neglected, and the other half is largely about Shakespeare's diction. I had already begun to devote my whole existence to the Bard, either acting or directing or writing or broadcasting or reviewing or God knows what.

I didn't get my fellowship the first time, but I got it my second time, in 1927. One had no obligation to teach or anything, though of course I did begin teaching soon after I got it. You simply had rooms in college and you had free run of the whole place and you were supposed to go on with your mathematics or your economics or whatever and then at the end of four years, you could possibly be given two more. Then you got into the whole machine of that and became a lecturer and examiner. I did more than twenty-five years as a teacher, tutor, bursar and steward. My life has been here. I've held most of the college offices. If you live long enough, often people will just let you stay on. You just become up on the shelf, but they don't dislodge you. After sixty years, they dare not.

I think they all went to live in Bloomsbury because there was a moment when the houses in Gordon Square were pretty inexpensive. At that moment, it was a reputable neighbourhood, and close to London University and so it was rather an intellectual affair. And they were rather beautiful houses, with a nice garden in the square, and quiet and pretty cheap, so when one lot moved there, they said, 'Come along, there's a house available'. So it grew, like a mushroom, more or less overnight.

I can't remember how much it cost exactly. What I do remember is that I had to live the whole year in London on about three hundred and fifty pounds. It was a struggle. I didn't get anything from the Hogarth Press. I was an apprentice, really. Leonard, on the whole, was stingy, parsimonious. But they were very poor, and they were just getting the whole thing going and then Leonard decided to buy up all the Freud papers, so that cost him a lot of money. That was when I was there, so I had the terrible experience, when I had only been there a few months, of being told to travel the books. So on a very wet day, with a suitcase, I took the books 'round. I went to one of the big bookshops in the City and after I'd been kept waiting a couple of hours, the manager said, 'Well, what have you got?' I took out the first volume of Freud's collected papers, and he said, 'We don't want any pornography here'. Bad beginning for a boy terrified of travelling and knowing he had to go back to Leonard without having sold anything. Fortunately, I then went on to Bumpers in Oxford, another great bookselling firm, and they had a manager who was very interested in the Hogarth Press and saw they were bringing out quite small editions of very interesting things, so he gave me a warm welcome and an order for twelve copies of poetry which nobody read then or after.

ANGELICA GARNETT

It's hard to admit, even now, that it took me so long to face the truth about myself, but the fact is that I had this long married life and four children and just so much in my life and then when I was living with my husband, he so weighed on me that I couldn't face it; I blocked it off. The result was that I just stayed in a kind of limbo for many years, like in a fairy story when people are put on a block of ice, or Rip Van Winkle. It's so long now since I've thought about my parents and their relationship. I don't think about it anymore, and I don't care about it, really.

Obviously, the person who was mainly responsible for my problems was Vanessa. Nobody did anything without her permission, or without knowing that she felt all right about it. She was a happy person – she hardly ever opened her mouth without making a joke. Yet it was all very ironical and I found that difficult when I was small because I always thought it was against me. (Irony very often is. It's a double-edged thing and it makes you feel defenceless so that you take things to heart, even when you aren't meant to.) When you are a child, an ironical remark is very hard to understand and the result of it is that it makes you very self-conscious – hyper-conscious of yourself – and you begin to criticize yourself. It means you can't let yourself go and just be natural. You become hypersensitive and awfully nervous.

I felt that way often as a child – very unsure of myself – and then when I got into my teens it was even worse. I was completely lost. I didn't know where I was or what to think or what to do. I hadn't any scale of values at all, really. *They* had values and they stuck to them but their values were too complicated for me. I didn't understand them, I think. It was too hyper-intelligent, or something. On paper, their values were really very good values. They didn't seek publicity or celebrity or think in terms of money either about themselves or their painting. They were very pure in that way. And they set immense value on work.

I'm sure that all my choices in my later life were unconsciously directed toward trying to please Vanessa and Duncan. A lot of the business of my trying to be a painter was really merely in order to please my parents. They were always very encouraging. They always tried to help me do whatever I said I wanted to do. I was a very bad painter for a very long time and it might have been better to have been able to say to myself, 'Well, look, this isn't any good. Why don't you try something else?'

If you're brought up by people like that, you're brought up so intelligently in a way that you become inhibited. I was shy anyway and all the permissiveness made me retire into myself still more. I was never enraged when I was a child. It was unthinkable because no one expected it and everyone got so distressed if you showed any tiny bit of anger that you felt you were destroying the people upon whom you most depended. If I had certain tantrums they would upset my mother so much that I felt I was doing something really ghastly, like murdering the very person I most depended on. This made all my rages go back inside me. I bottled them all up because I couldn't face doing that to my mother. I would have given anything for a nice open situation. I think one finds oneself much more quickly that way. You can trust a person who tells you what she thinks whereas my mother was also hypersensitive and felt she couldn't say everything she felt. She wasn't clear cut enough. She always wanted me to take the lead and to say what I wanted so she never said what she wanted. I was much too young to take such responsibility.

Vanessa was a very, very dominant person. She had an extremely strong personality. She was all-enveloping emotionally: very loving but so possessive. It was therefore extremely difficult to get out of her influence, particularly for me. She was so desperately enmeshed in Duncan that she thought I must be something wonderful because of that.

Vanessa was a very happy person as long as she felt protected. I think that's why Charleston existed – so that she could feel her own atmosphere around her. If she wasn't worried or apprehensive that something might happen which would destroy this delicious peace, as long as she was free to work and had her family around her – she loved family life – then she was happy and she could transmit a certain sort of happiness. She couldn't face the rough and tumble of the ordinary world – London, say, or Paris. She couldn't possibly have faced New York, not even in those days.

I think they were insensitive about other human beings. To me, this comes out in this one single fact: that my mother kept the knowledge from me as to who my father actually was. It seems to me very odd that they didn't think it was sufficiently important to tell me who my father was until I was seventeen. It just didn't tally with Vanessa's apparently liberated way of looking at life. I would have thought she should have told me and be damned to what people thought.

My mother told me at Charleston just after the death of my brother Julian. She was in a very emotional state of mind and perhaps thought that everything had got to come out and so she would tell me. I said as little as possible. It was too much to take in. She thought the nature of my affection for Duncan would change and perhaps it did, but it took a long time to show, I should think.

I have no doubt that going to live with my husband was an effort to escape from her. I became lovers with my husband and we lived together for two or three years before we got married: off and on, because it wasn't easy to find a place to live and his first wife was still around. But although I was quite a reasonable age when I married – I was about twenty-two

– I was still very much under the domination of my mother and I lived at Charleston because I hadn't got a place of my own and I hadn't got a job because I was trying to be a painter, so it was as though I was much younger.

I didn't have a happy marriage. I felt very guilty for having married my husband. I thought I never should have, but he had such a strong will that he could make one do whatever he wanted one to do. I felt that I was sinning against myself, that I would have done better not to have done it, and I think that is perfectly true. I still think it's true. I knew that my mother thought it was a bad idea, but that didn't make any impression on me because I was so longing to get away from her and she wasn't able to talk about it to me with any kind of objectivity and therefore what she said didn't make any impression on me at all. The fact that I was twenty-five years younger than my husband and that his relationship with my parents was so close made me feel as though they were three together and I was just one helpless creature out there alone, mesmerized by them. Whatever I did seemed to be wrong because it seemed to me as though my only choices were either to be with my parents or to be with Bunny and either way was wrong. I never thought of going out on my own and being all alone. It was just the beginning of the war and one couldn't do exactly what one liked or go where one wanted to go.

I suppose I was alienated from myself in a strange way, so I often didn't have the reactions one might expect me to have had. It was as though I were living in a completely artificial personality. I didn't really exist except to please other people, so when I married, my main aim in life was to please my husband. I had no wishes or inclinations of any serious kind of my own. He was very much in love with me. I suppose he hadn't tumbled to the fact that I was this strangely half-developed creature. He was very kind. He was a wonderful man, really. He would have been a wonderful friend to have had. It was just that he was the wrong husband, particularly for me, because of his past with my parents and the incestuousness of the whole thing. It was a frightfully bad idea for him to have married me and I think he should have known that.

My meetings with Vanessa were very painful for the most part. We pretended to get on very well but there were terrible silences when neither of us could think of what to say to the other. I could have asked her why she didn't tell me about Duncan being my father. If I had asked the right question, it probably would have broken the ice between us, and if we had got to talking about those things it would have been a tremendously liberating experience. It must have made her unhappy, too, because she adored me and she would have loved to have felt that there was a real living sympathy between us. Instead, it was a kind of dead area. It was as though we were two dead branches on a tree; we couldn't do anything more than just rustle in the wind. It was very, very sad. Perhaps I just didn't know how to love anybody. It's a sort of wisdom that is given one by being able to love people. I allowed myself to be frightened and petrified and frozen.

After my husband died, I surrounded myself with ghosts at Charleston and at moments I found that very hard to cope with. It's quite a good thing to live through that sort of thing, if you come out of it, but I very nearly didn't. I got ill. I thought I was desperately ill in some other way but it turned out to be a major depression. Duncan died, and I think it was partly due to that, but it was probably due to all sorts of other things, too. I think that years of repression had something to do with it. But I just carried on with my life – painting and doing the usual sorts of things. Quentin was living three or four miles away, so I saw a lot of them and I had people over to stay and my children came down to see me.

On holiday one year, I bought a house about a hundred kilometres from where I live now. It was a tiny cottage with two rooms. Since it was uninhabitable in winter, I would just go in the summers for three or four months to work on my book. I did that for two years and then the penny dropped that I really wanted to live in France rather than England. So on another holiday, I stopped here. I had got a passion for looking at empty houses and I went to the house agent and they showed me this house and it was the only one they had on their list of the kind of house that I wanted and within twenty-four hours I decided to buy it.

Once I got here, though, I had lots of black thoughts and often sort of slumped down saying, 'My God, what have I done? Did I do the right thing to come and live here?' This went on for about a year and then slowly, as I began to know people and feel more at home and as I got used to the French way of doing things I began to feel happier than I have ever been in my life. And now I'm doing sculpture that I absolutely adore doing.

There are certain people who think that Bloomsbury was too much of an elite and had all the faults of an elite; that it was a very small group of people who thought they were vastly superior to everyone else and that this was a very bad thing. There is some truth in that, and I can't make up my own mind whether I think it's a bad thing to be elitist or not. I think that if you have the luck to be a member of a small group like that there is something very good about it, as long as you don't exaggerate it. But there are people who won't accept that and one cannot make out whether they are justified in their criticism or whether they are simply suffering from having been excluded from Bloomsbury. There are quite a lot of people who would have loved, who would have reacted at once if they'd been asked to dinner or something, and who just can't bear the fact that they weren't asked.

The more I think about Bloomsbury, the more I respect their ideas. Every time, they seem to have been right. They obviously aren't perfect. Nobody is. I think their failures, such as they were, came mostly from a sort of emotional failure, a failure to quite realize what other people were thinking and feeling and their inability to express their emotions in any direct way so that you never quite knew what they were feeling and yet you always knew that there was something.

But I really had a very happy childhood. It creates a rather false picture to say that I was unhappy in childhood because I was repressed, because though there were things which I now regard as having been unfortunate because they had an unfortunate effect on my development, actually at the time I was extremely happy. It was lovely. I wasn't an only child, but I had more or less of an only child's upbringing because my brothers were so much older than I was. I enjoyed being spoiled. I loved having all those grownups fussing over me. It was just the pain and difficulty of getting out of that, when I was forced to grow up, that was the unhappy moment. That's true for everybody, more or

less. It's just that I was more spoiled than most people, so it was more painful.

I hanker for the world of my childhood because it was so utterly wonderful. It was the gaiety, the love of life, the sparkling intelligence about everything, the way they struck sparks off each other – at good moments, anyway – and the affection, the tremendous affection. One took it for granted. It was always there, and there seemed to be more of it, really, than I find in most people nowadays. Maybe that's partly because as a child, one is so intimate with people. You absorb them in a way that you don't when you're grown up. When you are born into a circle of people, because you're so small, you just absorb them, take everything in, without thinking about it, so you are obviously, naturally very intimate. You know people much better than you can possibly say you know them and so I suppose that's one of the things one misses. One never feels quite so intimate with anyone else again.

Nigel Nicolson was twelve years old when his parents, Harold Nicolson and Vita Sackville-West, purchased the fifteenth century crumbling compound known as Sissinghurst Castle for £12,375. It was uninhabitable, abandoned, but exceedingly romantic and there, in the Kent countryside, Nigel and his brother, Ben, grew up. Harold was often away – first abroad, as a diplomat, and then, when he became a Member of Parliament, in London. Vita remained at Sissinghurst with her garden and her writing, spending hours in the Tower, the four-storey look-out built in 1560 that she adopted as her workplace. The author of some forty books, as was her husband, Vita became best known as a popular romance novelist and garden writer. Her own garden on Sissinghurst's nearly seven acre estate is among the most famous in England. The year Vita died ten thousand visitors came to admire her and Harold's work. Last year 141,000 visitors came to see not only the garden, but also the preservation of the literary life of its creators: the dignified Harold Nicolson and the dramatic Sackville-West, whose connection with Bloomsbury and Virginia Woolf gives the place an added allure.

Ben became an art historian, Nigel a writer, editor, publisher and politician, serving seven years in the House of Commons. He founded the publishing company Weidenfeld and Nicolson in 1946. One of his two daughters is an editor there. His fifteen published books include a biography of Napoleon; a book of letters between himself and his son, Adam, while traversing America from opposite ends (meeting in the middle); and an intimate portrayal of his parents' unusual marriage: though each preferred lovers of their own gender, their devotion to and love for each other was profound. In 1973, he published the first of six volumes of Virginia Woolf's collected letters. He named the small study at Sissinghurst Castle where he did that work and where he continues to write, 'The Virginia Room'. He came to live at Sissinghurst permanently in 1962, when his mother died, and has lived there since. Harold died in 1968. The house and grounds, less living quarters for the Nicolson family, was handed over to the National Trust in 1967.

I'm the rural rustic son so I got to live in the house. Ben was the urban son. I was going to use the Tower as my room, but it was so full of my mother's books and I didn't want to disturb them and put in my own, and there were so many other rooms. So I left it just as it was when she died, with the addition of shades and coated glass to protect the books and heaters. My mother was impervious to cold. She never lit the fire. She might heat one bar of an electric heater when the temperature fell to twelve degrees below zero. She just piled blankets and rugs on her knees. She hated spending money on luxuries.

I kept everything as it was, even a painting of a naked boy riding a tiger. We called him Peter Scott, after a boy our age who was the son of the naturalist Geoffrey Scott with whom our mother had a brief affair. Vita told us that Peter's father would make him run around naked to make him hearty. She would hold this up to us as an example. We hated Peter Scott. One day – I must have been about eight – I stabbed him in the back with my sword. The painting was never mended.

I never felt intimidated by the success of my parents. I took it for granted. It wasn't as if they were in the top flight of fame: Harold and Vita didn't mean all that much to the schoolboys. There was just one terrible occasion with my grandmother when she wanted to do my mother a good turn. She sent a copy of Vita's novel *The Edwardians*, which had just been published, to every boy in the school, inscribing each copy with a little note that said, 'This comes to you with the compliments of Lady Sackville-West, the mother of the author and the grandmother of your two friends Ben and Nigel.' I was thirteen years old! It was mortifying.

I met all the Bloomsburys as a child. It was a big collection of aunts and uncles. It was fun for children because they were not dismissive of children and they were very active – they played tennis, bowls, took long walks. But it was Virginia I knew best, because she knew my mother. I first met Virginia when I was five years old. My recollection of her is that she was extraordinarily human and she was wonderful to children. She had no children of her own and she more or less adopted her nieces and nephews. 'Ah, Vita's two boys!' She had fun being with them without the responsibility. She wouldn't have made a good mother but she was a wonderful aunt and she was very exciting to us. Although we were less than ten years old, we knew she was a very famous woman: the best known novelist alive. We knew that. And so when she asked us about simple incidents in our lives and at school it was extraordinarily accurate. She would say, 'Now, what's the French mistress like?' And we would then in our little schoolboy ways attempt to describe this woman. And Virginia would say, 'No, no, no, that's not good enough. What colour are her eyes? What gestures does she make? Is she frightened of the class, or are you frightened of her?' She would force us to analyze it more deeply, but in a very humourous way. I remember she said to me once that nothing has really happened until it has been described.

Vanessa, on the other hand, was formidably alarming. I was terrified of her. I didn't, of course, meet her very much, because my mother found her equally alarming. Vanessa resented my mother's intrusion into Bloomsbury. Even at the age of twelve I felt the strain between them: Vanessa's cold stares of resentment. And I don't quite know why it was, but I think it could have been jealousy. She was intensely jealous of her sister and didn't want to share her sister with anybody else, in that sort of way.

My mother had a strong feminist streak for some reason. She refused to join my father when he was posted abroad with foreign legations and embassies. She would visit him but she wouldn't join him because if she had she would have been regarded simply as the wife of the Counsellor or the Ambassador or whatever and she refused to play that role. She had her own rare gifts and she wasn't going to sacrifice them even for the man she loved. And he absolutely supported her in this. The marriage was a very great success, except in the sexual way. In their mutual companionship, mutual support and absolute undying love for each other until the day she died it was the most productive marriage you could imagine.

They never quarrelled. I think my father would avoid subjects he knew would irritate Vita. He tended to sail with the prevailing winds and he had a light touch on the tiller. He was very sensitive, not only to her, but to other people's likely reactions and sensitivities. My parents wrote to each other every day when they were apart, and each kept all of the other's letters. The correspondence stretches for nearly fifty years. I think each wrote over ten thousand letters. In the beginning they were love letters, and in a way, they continued to be. My family was really knit together by correspondence, more than by conversation. They would write to us and we would write back to them and in this way we got to know each other far better by writing than by meeting. It seems sort of strange.

Vita was really rather shy. She reversed the normal process. Most people start off shy and then gain their self-confidence. With Vita, it was the other way around. In her youth she was immensely social and reckless to a point and then when she came here, when she was 38, she changed and became more of a recluse. She didn't want to know any more than a few intimate friends and didn't make new friends. She didn't travel. She would travel abroad, but she wouldn't go to London. When she was confronted by strangers she was awkward and longing for them to go away so she could be alone with her books. She was the same with her family to some extent, but mostly my father. She found it difficult to talk to him about his work, and then finding that she didn't know very much about him she grew more and more silent. She was actually, I think, unkind to him in that way. It put a lot of strain on us, and I think it was a bit unfair. She used to actually ask to be left alone with her sons, but we would beg my father to come down with us because we did not want to be alone with her, simply because she would relapse into total silence at dinner.

She didn't have much laughter. She didn't have the wit or cleverness my father did. She had a great gift for storytelling, but she despised novels. She wanted to be remembered as a poet. Some of her books weren't bad novels but she felt she was a bad novelist. But she wasn't. She wasn't as original a novelist as Virginia was, of course. Virginia invented a whole new way of telling stories through this stream of consciousness. She once said that Vita wrote schoolgirl stories. But Vita did once write a short novel called *Seducers in Ecuador*, which she wrote very, very quickly in the evenings when she was on a walking tour with my father. It is far and away the most brilliant of Vita's books and Virginia did become jealous – just with that one book. Vita wrote *Seducers* in the evenings in the inns and my father wrote *Sun People* at the same time.

My father was a very funny man and a wonderful talker and storyteller and conversationalist and very elegant.

I was influenced very much by my father, and very little by my mother. She only ever communicated with us about trivialities. My father was the opposite. He would talk about anything, and he would initiate conversations. We could confide in my father. But there was one thing we never talked about in our family:

we never talked about sex. Of course, in their case, it was even more difficult for them to talk to their children about their own experiences, so it was taboo. It was never, never mentioned.

I wasn't very close to Vita, and I regret it now. She didn't establish an intimacy with either of her sons. It was never awkward. I just would never confide in her and now I think she would have welcomed it. She wrote a letter to Harold that I only read after her death and in which she says that she felt a failure as a mother. That struck home. I felt very guilty. I knew it wasn't her fault, but mine. It was my responsibility as well as hers. She was very private about her writing. She never talked about it, so we never asked questions. We never knew the titles of her books except when they were advertised and never knew the subject unless we read the book. I got to know more about her feelings through her published writing than I did by talking with her. I was the conventional son and I brought up my own children like I was brought up. Adam complains about it. He tells me what a bad father I was. He says I have no warmth. He'll live here when I die, with his wife and children. He doesn't like the 'Castle' part of the address: says it's too hoity-toity.

This book is dedicated to
my designer, Mary Shanahan,
to whom I humbly apologise.
A.MCW.

The dust jacket text was composed in handset monotype Deepdene by M & H Type, San Francisco, California. The body text was photoset in Bembo by Wenham Arts, Peterborough, England. Alen MacWeeney used a Rolleiflex and a Pentax 645 camera. The photographs were made on 120 size colour negative film and printed on Kodak paper by Carol Fondé in New York City. The colour separations were undertaken by Balding & Mansell plc, Wisbech, England. The book was printed on 150 gsm matt cream Parilux and endpapered with 135 gsm Colorplan by Balding & Mansell. The endpapered book blocks were bound by Hunter & Foulis, Edinburgh, Scotland.